THE PERFORMING ARTS

Other books in this series include:

Military Uniforms
Carol Harris and Mike Brown

Accessories
Carol Harris and Mike Brown

Children's Costumes
Carol Harris and Mike Brown

Women's Costumes
Carol Harris and Mike Brown

Men's Costumes
Carol Harris and Mike Brown

Festivals
Ellen Galford

North American Dress
Dr. Louise Aikman

Ceremonial Costumes
Lewis Lyons

Everyday Dress
Chris McNab

Rescue Services
Carol Harris and Mike Brown

Religious Costumes
Ellen Galford

TWENTIETH-CENTURY DEVELOPMENTS IN FASHION AND COSTUME

THE PERFORMING ARTS

ALYCEN MITCHELL

MASON CREST PUBLISHERS

www.masoncrest.com

Mason Crest Publishers Inc.
370 Reed Road
Broomall, PA 19008
(866) MCP-BOOK (toll free)
www.masoncrest.com

First printing 2002

1 2 3 4 5 6 7 8 9 10

Library of Congress Cataloging-in-Publication Data available

ISBN 1-59084-426-2

Printed and bound in Malaysia

Editorial and design by
Amber Books Ltd.
Bradley's Close
74–77 White Lion Street
London N1 9PF

Project Editor: Marie-Claire Muir
Designer: Zoe Mellors
Picture Research: Lisa Wren

Picture Credits:
Popperfoto: 5 (left and bottom right), 6, 9, 10, 13, 16, 18, 22, 23, 27, 31, 47, 54, 56, 58–59.
Topham: 5 (top), 8, 15, 20, 25, 28, 33, 34, 35, 38, 40, 44–45, 46, 48, 49, 51, 52.

Cover images: Popperfoto: background. **Topham:** main, top, and bottom.

Acknowledgment:
For authenticating this book, the Publishers would like to thank
JONES NEW YORK

Contents

Introduction   7

Chapter 1   9
The Movies

Chapter 2   23
The World of Dance

Chapter 3   35
Stage and Theater

Chapter 4   49
Circus Fun and Vaudeville

Glossary   60

Timeline   62

Further Information   63

Index   64

Introduction

Every day we go to our closets with the same question in mind: what shall I wear today? Clothing can convey status, wealth, occupation, religion, sexual orientation, and social, political, and moral values. The clothes we wear affect how we are perceived and also reflect what image we want to project.

Fashion has always been influenced by the events, people, and places that shape society. The 20th century was a period of radical change, encompassing two world wars, suffrage, a worldwide Depression, the invention of "talkies" and the rise of Hollywood, the birth of the teenager, the global spread of television, and, later, the World Wide Web, to name just a few important developments. Politically, economically, technologically, and socially, the world was changing at a fast and furious pace. Fashion, directly influenced by all these factors, changed with them, leaving each period with its fashion icon.

The 1920s saw the flapper reign supreme, with her short dress and cropped, boyish hair. The '30s and '40s brought a wartime mindset: women entered the workforce en masse and traded their silk stockings for nylon. During the conservative 1950s—typified by twin sets and capri pants—a young Elvis Presley took the world by storm. The '60s gave us PVC, miniskirts, and mods, and in 1967, the Summer of Love spawned a new language of fashion in which bell-bottoms and tie-dyed shirts became political expressions of peace and love. In the 1980s, power and affluence became the hallmarks of a new social group, the yuppies. Designer branding led the way, and the slogan "Nothing comes between me and my Calvins" started an era of status dressing. The 1990s will be best remembered for a new fashion word introduced by the underground street and music movement of Seattle, grunge.

Twentieth-Century Developments in Fashion and Culture is a 12-volume, illustrated series that looks at changing fashions throughout this eventful century, and encourages readers to question what the clothes they wear reveal about themselves and the world they live in.

Special introduction and consultation:
JONES NEW YORK

CHAPTER 1

The Movies

From the beginning of the 20th century, people have been copying fashions they have seen on film. What we wear and how we look have been more widely influenced by the movies and their stars than by any other field in the performing arts.

We have all heard it said that imitation is the sincerest form of flattery. Well, it is a rare person who would not want to look like a movie star. Two of the earliest movie stars to have an impact on fashion were Lillian Gish and Mary Pickford. As fragile as a bird, Lillian Gish was one of the silent-film era's most gifted dramatic actresses, while Mary

This 1930s actress (left) is dressed in a bias-cut gown. Her eye makeup helps create a vamp look. Clara Bow (right), the original "It Girl," created her flapper image with a bobbed haircut and makeup.

Pickford had an old-fashioned quality that earned her the nickname "America's Sweetheart." Both played up their girlish looks on screen by styling their hair in loose curly ringlets and wearing delicate lace dresses.

If silent stars, such as Gish and Pickford, were demure innocents, then Pola Negri and Gloria Swanson were exotic temptresses. In the 1920s, sultry female characters who led men to their ruin or death were called vamps. The word *vamp* was first used to describe Theda Bara's vampire-like character in the silent film *A Fool There Was* (1915). Bara, the original vamp, was born in

Roy Rogers, the yodeling cowboy star, liked his fancy duds. He was more of a country-and-western fashion icon than an authentic ranch hand.

COWBOYS IN COSTUME

From Tom Mix in the silent-movie era to Clint Eastwood today, cowboys in Westerns have not changed their outfits much over the years. Jeans, denim jackets, short leather coats, flannel shirts, and **chaps** are all features of the cowboy style. Their pants had a slight flare to accommodate their plain, thick-heeled boots with **spurs**. They wore wide-brimmed hats with a crease down the middle. They tied bandannas around their necks and wore guns in holsters at their hips. In fact, the clothes in Westerns are so closely based on outfits worn by real working cowboys that they were among the most authentic costumes in the movies.

Of course, "rhinestone cowboys," such as musical star Roy Rogers and his wife Dale Evans, are exceptions. Their glitzy cowboy outfits were closer to stage costumes than genuine cowboy clothes, owing much to the influence of country and western musicians at the Grand Ole Opry or to Broadway musicals set on the plains like *Oklahoma!*

Cincinnati, Ohio, and her real name was Theodosia Goodman. However, Fox Studios put it about that *Theda Bara* was an anagram for *Arab death* and that she was the love child of a French painter and an Egyptian dancer. During World War I, Bara acted her seductive way through over 40 silent films.

Vamps like Bara, Swanson, and Negri dressed in sensational costumes with a sensual flavor of the exotic East. They wore jeweled turbans, and their eyes smoldered beneath heavy black kohl makeup, while they smoked cigarettes from long holders.

Silent-film heartthrob Rudolph Valentino was the male equivalent of the vamp. Nicknamed the "Latin lover," Valentino played a series of irresistible seducers of women. His most famous role was that of a handsome Arab sheik.

The last great silent star to influence fashion was Clara Bow. Her rise to fame was meteoric, and for a brief moment during the mid-1920s she was "America's It Girl." Bow even made a silent film called *It* (1927). What was "it"? In a word (or two)—sex appeal.

The uninhibited Bow personified party-loving youth after World War I. Her hair was cut in a short, sassy bob, and her Cupid's-bow mouth was painted with bright lipstick. She wore short **shift** dresses that shimmied when she danced. This exuberant young **hedonist** was the ultimate flapper of the Roaring Twenties. Women were fascinated by her liberated ways and imitated her look. Scandal, followed by a nervous breakdown and the arrival of talkie films in 1927, ended her short career.

1930s

During the early 1930s, women's fashions were becoming more streamlined and tailored. Fashion designers started to cut their material across the woven grain, a technique known as **bias cutting**. This helped them create a new form-

CARY GRANT AND THE TUXEDO

Cary Grant's seemingly effortless grace and elegance made him one of the greatest screen idols of all time. Although he always looked suave and debonair regardless of what he wore, nothing is more quintessentially Grant than the relaxed sophistication of the tuxedo.

During the 1930s, men wore the tuxedo as casual eveningwear—when they went dancing, for example. Long tailcoats with stiff wing-collar shirts were reserved for important evening events. Grant made the tailcoat look dated and stuffy. He helped the tuxedo replace tails as formal eveningwear once and for all.

Katharine Hepburn preferred pants and penny loafers to glittering gowns and high heels off camera. Her timeless, sporty style is still highly influential.

fitting look that was used primarily for dresses, especially evening gowns. Bias-cut garments were incredibly comfortable and figure-hugging at the same time. Hollywood movie stars, both on and off camera, played a large part in promoting what became the dominant fashion trend of the decade.

Few Hollywood stars of the 1930s could resist the flattering look of bias-cut dresses. The star most associated with this trend, however, was Jean Harlow. In such films as *Dinner at Eight* (1933), Harlow's satin evening gowns fit like a second skin. The stark perfection of Harlow's bias-cut dresses left audiences breathless.

The costume designer responsible for Harlow's slinky look was Adrian. Chief costume designer at MGM Studios, Adrian started his career designing costumes for Broadway shows. From the late 1920s to the early 1940s, Adrian was the driving force behind the image of such stars as Dolores Del Rio, both on and off camera. He created Greta Garbo's slouch hat in the film *A Woman of Affairs* (1928), which became popular among women in the early 1930s. He was also responsible for the lacy hair net at the nape of Heddy Lamarr's neck in *I Take This Woman* (1939). Known as a **snood**, it became a popular hair accessory in the 1940s.

However, Adrian is best remembered for his work with movie star Joan Crawford. Adrian gave Crawford's costumes big, padded shoulders to minimize her big hips. They became her signature look, and they had a huge influence on the American profile of the late 1930s and 1940s, especially with tailored suits. When he put Crawford in a sheer white gown with ruffled sleeves for the film *Letty Lynton* (1932), Adrian started a fashion trend. His dress was so widely copied at the time that Crawford was called the most imitated woman in the world—Macy's department store alone reported selling over 500,000 replicas.

Before the 1930s, few women dared wear pants in the streets. However, following the lead of more liberated movie stars, such as Greta Garbo, Marlene Dietrich, and Katharine Hepburn, pants were no longer regarded as eccentric or shocking, and they were increasingly featured as women's leisurewear.

Hepburn, in particular, usually preferred to wear pants off camera. She also adopted other traditional menswear, including Shetland sweaters, tweed blazers, **brogues**, and long cardigans with pockets. In private life, Hepburn wore little or no makeup. Her sporty elegance impressed many American women at the time. For them, Hepburn symbolized the free-spirited independence to which they aspired. Hepburn's style was the precursor of the *Annie Hall* look of the 1980s.

1940s & 1950s

In 1939, Vivien Leigh looked so attractive as Scarlett O'Hara in *Gone with the Wind*, it must have been hard for Clark Gable to say the famous line, "Frankly, my dear, I don't give a damn." As the world's most famous Southern belle, the

HUMPHREY BOGART AND THE TRENCH COAT

Thanks to the way Humphrey Bogart wore one in such movies as *The Maltese Falcon* (1941), the trench coat and the detective are irrevocably linked in filmgoers' minds. Originally, troops wore them in the trenches. Then, after World War I, they were used as a raincoat or topcoat. Traditional trench coats are buff-colored and made of cotton or wool with a belt at the waist, **epaulets**, and a flap at the shoulders. In detective films, Bogart wore his trench coat with the collar turned up and the belt tied instead of buckled. Nonchalantly stylish as the world-weary private eye, Bogart ensured that the trench coat became a fashion classic.

By the late 1950s, such formal outfits as these, inspired by Scarlett's sumptuous gowns in the film *Gone With the Wind*, were going out of fashion, especially among the younger generation. Youths created their own casual beatnik style.

English actress wore the full **crinoline** dresses of the American Civil War era. Scarlett's gowns would have a huge impact on clothing after World War II. Tops were fitted and skirts were full. Nostalgia for mid-19th-century fashions was the main foundation upon which the elegant look of the 1950s was built.

Carmen Miranda is permanently fixed in audiences' minds as the star with the tutti-frutti hat. Nicknamed the "Brazilian Bombshell," during World War II, Miranda starred in a series of lively Technicolor musicals with Latin American themes. In her song-and-dance numbers, Miranda wore a fruit-covered turban, cropped, off-the-shoulder tops, and floor-length skirts. Although her costumes were always outrageous—lavish amounts of gold **lamé**, plenty of jewelry, and, of course, an abundance of fruit—they were actually based on the clothes of fruit sellers in the Brazilian markets.

Off camera, Miranda loved flashy platform-soled shoes. She wore less extravagant turbans with suits and lounging robes, which helped make the turban a popular wartime alternative to the hat. She also sparked a taste for costume jewelry, often made of bright red, green, orange, and yellow Bakelite plastic with bold tropical themes.

Long after many Hollywood actresses faded from the limelight, the World War II starlet Veronica Lake continued to be famous, chiefly for her hairstyle. She wore her long, wavy hair loosely cascading over her shoulder in the gangster film *This Gun for Hire* (1942). Nicknamed the peek-a-boo look because Lake's hair tumbled over one eye in publicity shots, it was the last word in glamour, and every woman wanted her hairstyle. Worried that women

JAMES DEAN, THE REBEL HERO IN T-SHIRT AND JEANS

The movie *Rebel without a Cause* (1955) made James Dean a star. In the film, about teenagers angry at society, Dean dressed in jeans and a t-shirt, with a plain zip-up jacket. It became the uniform of rebel youth and the rock 'n' roll musicians they admired. A bit of a **beatnik**, Dean dressed this way in his private life. Dean had a "live for the moment" attitude to life, and his untimely death in a car crash in 1955 turned him into a cult figure.

doing war work might get their hair caught in factory machinery, the government asked Lake to change her hair to a tied-back style.

The most important Hollywood costume designer of the postwar era was Edith Head. Chief designer at Paramount Pictures from 1938 to 1967, Head also worked for other film studios. Throughout her long career, she designed clothes for some of the biggest names in Hollywood, including Mae West, Marlene Dietrich, Elizabeth Taylor, and Grace Kelly. It was Head who first put Dorothy Lamour in her famous sarong in the film *The Jungle Princess* (1936) and dressed Gloria Swanson for her comeback in the disturbing portrait of Hollywood, *Sunset Boulevard* (1950).

During the 1950s, ladylike elegance was a predominant theme throughout fashion. Hats and gloves were a fashion-must again, and everything had to coordinate, right down to the last button. Grooming

Grace Kelly, shown here with husband, Prince Rainer of Monaco, in the 1960s, is wearing a simple yet elegant dress, with her hair neatly pulled back.

and formality were the order of the day, which made women look sophisticated and mature.

No movie star epitomized this ladylike look more than Grace Kelly. Even when she was relaxing at home, Kelly always looked immaculately polished. Plain white shirts, swing coats, calf-length skirts, cashmere **twin sets**, and pearls were all hallmarks of the Kelly style. Her name is closely linked with Hermès, a French leather goods and accessories company. She helped popularize their chic silk scarves in America, where they were prized for their effortless refinement. When Kelly married Prince Rainier of Monaco, Hermès named a handbag in her honor. The Kelly bag became the most desired fashion accessory of the decade. Even today, long after her death, Grace Kelly continues to be a fashion icon who inspires us.

BOHEMIAN CHIC

Audrey Hepburn offered a more bohemian version of Kelly's sophisticated and ladylike look. Half-Dutch and half-British, Hepburn was originally a ballet dancer. She took the "Left Bank" look of the artistic quarter of Paris and made it chic in America. By the mid-1950s, she was a hugely popular movie star.

Hepburn's off-camera clothes were always simple as well as elegant. Her signature look included big sunglasses, black turtleneck sweaters, slim, cropped slacks, and ballet slipper-style pumps. She also created a fashion for wearing shirts unbuttoned at the bottom and tied at the waist. Her clothes emphasized her elfin haircut and slender figure. People used the word *gamine* to describe her, which means street urchin or tomboy in French. The beatniks—jazz- and poetry-loving young intellectuals and students of the era—picked up elements of her look. Like Kelly, Hepburn is now a timeless role model.

Another European star who dressed in "Left Bank" fashions was French actress Brigitte Bardot. Bardot had also originally trained as a ballerina. Her long hair with bangs and her high ponytail were popular with beatnik girls.

However, it was her frilly gingham bikinis and gingham dresses with scoop necklines and full skirts that had the greatest effect on audiences.

RETRO TRENDS

Berets are one of those indispensable fashion accessories that have appeared over and over again throughout the 20th century. They were particularly popular between World War I and World War II. Faye Dunaway revived the beret when she played a gun-toting 1930s moll in the film *Bonnie and Clyde* (1967). With her beret worn to one side, Dunaway looked so stylish that she was widely copied in the late 1960s and early '70s. The retro outfits in *Bonnie and Clyde* also anticipated the influence that 1930s fashions would have on 1970s clothing design.

Two years later, Ali McGraw brought youthful, collegiate style to the screen in *Love Story* (1970). McGraw's character in the film is a "flower child" who falls for a boy from a wealthy, conservative background at an Ivy League college. *Love Story* was incredibly romantic, and after seeing the

When Faye Dunaway played a glamorous 1930s bank robber on the run in *Bonnie and Clyde*, the beret came back into vogue.

movie, many girls wanted to look and be just like McGraw. They adopted her ponchos, crocheted shawls, bell bottoms, floppy hats, and knitted scarves, as well as her long breezy hair with a central part.

The zany clothes in the movie *Annie Hall* (1977) kick-started one of the major trends of the early 1980s. American fashion designer Ralph Lauren created Diane Keaton's outfits in the film. Keaton dressed in loose, baggy clothes, including brogues, pleated pants, men's shirts, vests, and oversized jackets. A witty reinterpretation of 1930s and 1940s menswear, the look was finished with a short tie and a fedora hat pulled down over the forehead. The *Annie Hall* look was easy for women to re-create cheaply using secondhand men's clothes.

More recently, *Moulin Rouge* (2001), set in Paris in the late 19th century, led to a corset revival, but these were for show instead of shape. Made of rich satins and silk in deep shades, such as sapphire, amethyst, and crimson, they were promoted by fashion designers as eveningwear. Nicole Kidman, star of the movie, encouraged the look by wearing corsets to evening events.

ACTRESSES AT THE ACADEMY AWARDS

When Jane Gaynor won the first Oscar for Best Actress in 1929, the Academy Award ceremony was a relatively low-key affair. In those days, ladies and gentlemen dressed in the same elegant evening clothes they would wear to a formal dinner-dance. However, once television brought the Oscars to the public, the event turned into a fashion extravaganza. As the stars started wearing more and more outrageous gowns to the ceremonies, they received negative coverage in the media. They finally wised up in the early 1990s. Now, most stars employ professional outfit coordinators, known as stylists, to help them make the right impression on the night of the awards. These days, it is rare to see a gross fashion blunder at the ceremonies.

CHAPTER 2

The World of Dance

From ballroom dancers to hip-hop artists on the street, dancers influenced fashion throughout the 20th century. Inspired by their glamorous costumes and freedom of movement, people have even adopted as casualwear clothes traditionally worn in the dance studio.

Isadora Duncan was the first dancer to have a noticeable effect on clothing in the early 1900s. An American pioneer of modern dance, Duncan broke away from the traditional moves of classical ballet, such as the **pirouette**.

Several 1950s movies stars, including Jean Simmons (left), began their careers as ballet dancers. Their graceful appearance was fashionable at the time. Modern-dance pioneer Isadora Duncan (right) wears a Grecian-style robe.

23

TYPICAL EARLY 20TH-CENTURY DANCEWEAR

In the early 1900s, most women wore evening gowns when they went out dancing. Like contemporary daytime dresses, these were fitted down to the hips with full, floor-length skirts, but evening gowns had short sleeves and off-the-shoulder necklines. Evening gowns were also covered with more lace, bows, and frills. Women decorated their swept-up hair with jewels, feathers, and floral sprays. They accessorized their gowns with long white gloves and tiny bags that held cards on which they recorded their partners' names for the various dances of the evening. Today, when we see pictures of women dancing to the waltzes popular at the time, we grow nostalgic for a more refined age. However, as enchanting as those gowns look, they must have been difficult to dance in. Not only were the gowns weighty and cumbersome, but women also wore tight corsets underneath them to make their waists smaller.

Duncan and other modern dancers believed that dancers should move naturally and freely to music, which influenced the clothes she chose to wear while dancing. Duncan made a name for herself in London and Paris before moving on to greater fame.

Duncan was introduced to Parisian audiences by another American pioneer of modern dance, Loie Fuller. At the time, Fuller's dancing was the talk of Paris. She fascinated audiences with the sinuous way she moved, her skirts swirling as she danced. An inspiration to artists, Fuller's dancing is associated with the **Art Nouveau** style, which is characterized by swaying lines and tendril **motifs**. Fuller's idealized image was depicted in countless designs, from posters to lamp bases and jewelry. The Art Nouveau style dominated Western design from 1890 to 1910.

Duncan's costumes created as much sensation as her experimental dancing. Instead of the conventional **tutu**, she wore flowing dresses inspired by ancient Greek robes, which allowed her to move freely. Duncan daringly rejected ballet slippers to dance barefoot, a practice now associated with modern dance. Her frequent appearances in European capital cities helped promote a trend toward looser, more comfortable clothes for women.

THE ORIENTAL INFLUENCE

Loie Fuller and Isadora Duncan were not the only dancers to travel to Paris to establish their careers. For the first half of the 20th century, Paris was

MATA HARI

Mata Hari, meaning "eye of the dawn," was the stage name of Dutch dancer Magaretha Gertrud Zelle. In her youth, Mata Hari lived in Southeast Asia, where she often watched Javanese dancing. What she saw inspired her to develop a dance routine that made her famous. She went to Paris in 1905, where, assuming the persona of a Javanese princess, her sensual moves and scanty costumes gained her huge notoriety. Her exotic headdress, jeweled bikini top, and swirling skirt of pearl beads became the standard costume of Oriental seductresses for the next two decades. Her contribution to dance and fashion is totally overshadowed by her exploits during World War I, which led to her execution as a German spy.

the cultural capital of the world, the place to be if you were a performer, a musician, an artist, or a designer. Fuller and Duncan paved the way for a Russian ballet company that had a huge impact on fashion just before and after World War I.

When the Ballets Russes came to Paris in 1909, no one had ever seen anything like it before. The beautiful Arabian costumes and sets Leon Bakst designed for dancers fueled a new taste for Oriental exoticism. The Ballets Russes created a trend for **harem pants**, kimono coats, turbans, and sumptuous jewelry. It popularized rich fabrics, such as heavy satins, embroidered silks, thick velvet, and gold lamé, as well as bold prints. The dazzling costumes made the pastel shades fashionable since the 1890s appear dated. Suddenly, fashionable women wanted to wear jewel-like colors, such as orange, turquoise, and violet, often in vivid combinations.

Parisian fashion designer Paul Poiret played an important role in promoting clothing influenced by the Oriental designs of the Ballets Russes. He gave lavish parties to publicize his version of the Eastern look, including the **lampshade dress** and the **hobble skirt**. At first, only high-society women and leading entertainers wore these exotic fashions. However, the trend was widely reported, and soon, anybody with any claim to style wanted to be part of it.

One well-known dancer, Irene Castle, gave these exotic fashions a twist that was very much her own. Irene, an American, and her English husband Vernon were a celebrated professional ballroom dance team in the years leading up to World War I. The Castles first delighted audiences in Paris. When they came to New York, their performances and teaching sessions brought them even wider acclaim. The couple popularized such dances as the turkey trot, the one-step, and the tango. Irene in her stylish dresses and Vernon in his tails were the original role models for ballroom dance teams throughout the 20th century.

Irene Castle adapted the Oriental fashions to her own dancing needs. She used fluid, floaty fabrics and shortened the hems to ankle length. Her favorite profile was one not too closely fitted. She turned the lampshade dress into a soft tunic effect with folds over the hips, and draped and slit the hobble skirt for ease of movement. Many of Irene's outfits were specially made for her at fashion designer Lucile's New York branch. Irene's stylish clothes had an influence on women's dress all over the United States. They soon widely copied her caps, buckle shoes, and velvet headbands trimmed with pearls. She was one of the first women to crop her hair in a short bob, and this, coupled with her willowy figure, led Irene to exude a new type of beauty that became associated with the 1920s flapper look.

BETWEEN THE WARS: PARTY TIME

Following World War I, the 1920s were a period when all that people seemed to want to do was party. It was a way of forgetting the wartime horrors they had witnessed and making up for their lost youth. Cocktail drinking was the latest craze, as was dancing to jazz. Dizzy young flappers supposedly spent all their time doing the Charleston. Along with other energetic dances popular in the 1920s, the Charleston helped raise hemlines to the knee. Typical dancing dresses were simple, sleeveless tubes decorated with **diamanté** beads or fringes, which shimmied as the dancer moved.

Like jazz, most of the dances popular in the 1920s had Afro-American origins. Josephine Baker was the most successful

Captured at the height of her career, jazz-age legendary dancer Josephine Baker is shown in her infamous miniscule banana loincloth and enormous jewels. Note the earrings, bangles, and anklets.

dancer of the era. Baker got her start in black song-and-dance revues in New York, but the real turning point in her career came in 1925, when she arrived in Paris. The French capital had fallen in love with jazz, and to the French, Baker was the living embodiment of its wild rhythms. At the height of her career, she was the highest-paid entertainer in Europe. Baker fell for France the way the French fell for her. She remained there for the rest of her life.

Baker brought an African flavor to contemporary fashion. Known for her bold jewelry, she popularized big bangles, anklets, beads, and necklets. She created a fashion for bobs with bangs and another for brightly dyed leather gloves. She scandalized conservative society with her outrageous and minuscule costumes. In one show, she wore nothing but pearls and a loincloth covered with jeweled bananas.

When it comes to dancing, Fred Astaire and Ginger Rogers are household names even today. They appeared in a series of romantic movies during the 1930s in which their stunning ballroom displays helped take peoples' minds away from the harsh realities of the **Depression** and political uncertainty in Europe. Astaire in his dashing evening clothes and Rogers in her trademark frilly gowns were

One of the greatest dance partnerships of all time, Fred Astaire and Ginger Rogers still inspire dancers today. Fred Astair was closely associated with the "Top Hat, White Tie, and Tails," and in one of his movies sang and danced to a song of that title.

SPANISH AND LATIN AMERICAN DANCERS' COSTUMES

Americans and Europeans embraced the sultry Latino tango in the early 1900s, and the tango made them receptive to other Hispanic rhythms and moves. The heel-stamping sound of the flamenco was soon heard in variety shows and song-and-dance revues at nightclubs. The dancers wore colorful, ruffled skirts and flounced blouses with low necklines derived from Gypsy costumes. The Gypsy dancer look, now associated with Latin American, as well as Spanish dancing, inspired European fashion designers, such as Cristóbal Balenciaga in the 1950s and Yves Saint Laurent in the 1970s.

icons of glamour and sophistication. They made ballroom dancing look spontaneous and easy, although their routines had actually taken months to prepare. Always graceful and elegant, Astaire and Rogers picked up where the Castles left off. In fact, they paid tribute to the Castles in their last film together, *The Story of Vernon and Irene Castle* (1939).

While Astaire and Rogers wowed movie audiences, Martha Graham and her revolutionary modern dance company were making waves on the New York stage. Graham developed a system of movement and a method of muscle control that remain cornerstones of today's modern dance. Her techniques are routinely taught in dance schools all over the world. In the 1930s and 1940s, Graham worked with leading progressive artists of the day, such as sculptor Isamu Noguchi and composer Aaron Copland. She had a traditional ballerina's physique, which contrasted not only with her dancing, but also with the unstructured dresses she wore during performances. Like Duncan before her, Graham danced barefoot. She was so influential that her image and style became what audiences expected to see when they went to a modern dance performance.

The black and Hispanic musicians who played the dance tunes were often snappy dressers with a unique style of their own. During the late 1930s and 1940s, some picked up on a fashion that had traveled from South America to New York and other cities. Known as a zoot suit, it consisted of a colorful, knee-length jacket with big, padded shoulders and a narrow waist, worn with generously pleated trousers that tapered sharply below the knee. The look was accessorized with a broad-brimmed hat and pointed-toe shoes.

DANCEWEAR MEETS DAYWEAR

A new generation of dancers pushed back the boundaries of modern dance in the 1960s and 1970s. The most celebrated of these dancers, Twlya Tharp, had an innovative, energetic style that incorporated jazz, tap, ballet, and modern dance. She performed to a wide range of music, from classical and contemporary to jazz and pop. In contrast with most ballerinas and modern dancers, Tharp had a short hairstyle with bangs. She surprised and delighted audiences by choosing to wear clothing usually reserved for the rehearsal studio during performances, such as wraparound sweaters, footless bodysuits, and leg warmers. This look helped kick-start a fashion for using dance clothing as leisurewear. Leg warmers, especially, were all the rage in the latter half of the 1970s and early 1980s. Women put them over jeans, tucked them into boots, and wore them under long skirts.

DISCO STYLE

By the mid-1970s, people were growing tired of wearing hippie clothes and "letting it all hang out" when they danced at rock and folk festivals. A taste for glamour reasserted itself. A new and exciting type of nightclub was springing up in major cities. Disco is the shortened term for *discotheque*, deriving from the French word for library, *bibliotheque*. Instead of having live dance bands, discos played the latest tunes from a "library" of records selected by a knowledgeable

BALLERINA'S TUTUS

The ballerina's tutu has its origins in the 19th century. There are two types of tutu. Both have skirts made of layers of **tulle**, or net, and are usually white. The first has a draped, knee- to calf-length skirt, which is fully gathered at the waist. The second has a short skirt stiffened so that it stands very straight, almost horizontal. Ballerinas wear special satin slippers known as pointe shoes, which have a hard, reinforced toe that enable them to dance on the tips of their toes; they are tied with ribbon ankle straps.

During the 1950s, the ballerina's dainty appearance corresponded with the taste for ladylike fashions. British ballet star Margot Fonteyn was considered one of the decade's more stylish dressers. The idealized likeness of a ballerina with little jewels on her skirt was a popular design for brooches and charms. Full skirts that reached just above the ankle were often referred to as ballerina skirts.

disc jockey, or DJ. The format was easy to copy, and by the late 1970s, discomania was sweeping Europe and America.

The disco sound had a vibrant beat. You could find your own groove or put together clever moves, but whichever way you sliced it, dressing up was part of the routine. There was usually a strict dress code—chic eveningwear was a must.

Disco dancers loved anything colorful and shiny. Satin came back into fashion in such colors as lime green, soda pink, and Day-Glo orange. Sequins and diamanté were sprinkled liberally on clothing. Women put sparkles all over their bodies and lip gloss on their mouths. They wore silk flowers in their hair and metallic polish on their nails. Stretchy clothes were made especially for dancing: slinky **jersey** dresses, jumpsuits, stretch jeans, and leotards with wraparound skirts. Many of the clothes spawned by disco were an homage to the fashions of the 1930s. In fact, Halston, the best-known fashion designer of the era, acknowledged that his clothes were inspired by those stylish years.

Discos were not just showcases for extravagant finery for women. The disco era made it fashionable for men to wear silk shirts and tight-fitting flares. John Travolta's sharp white suit in the blockbuster movie *Saturday Night Fever* (1977) is a symbol of the era. The disco group The Commodores took the trend to an extreme, wearing shiny space-age costumes.

Disco's flashy influence soon spread to daywear. People were so proud of their dancing clothes that they started wearing them on the streets. Eventually, overexposure tarnished the glamour, and by the mid-1980s, disco dancing and the fashions that went with it were out-of-date. However, its legacy revived an interest in dancing and dance music.

DANCING IN THE STREET

New types of moves began percolating up from city streets and into music video on television. Several Hollywood musical films, such as *Fame* (1980) and *Flashdance* (1983), brought street dancing to mainstream audiences. The dancers' appearance

Break-dancers, such as this member of the Hip Hop Nation dance troupe, originally performed their athletic moves on the streets in the 1980s. Their track suit-and-sneaker look is now an integral part of contemporary hip-hop culture.

in these movies excited people almost as much as their athletic movements. They wore sweatshirts off the shoulder, showing a tank top underneath and created a trend for leggings and cutoff t-shirts, a look that was soon worn as leisurewear.

The dancing in these movies was inspired by the extraordinary footwork, backspins, and dives—dubbed break dancing by the media—practiced and performed by black and Hispanic youths on the streets of American cities, such as New York. Performers—mainly but not exclusively boys—preferred calling their moves hip-hop dancing.

Because of the athletic nature of their dancing, these dancers dressed in sportswear and tracksuits. By the 1990s, this had evolved into a distinct look that made up the hip-hop style. Baggy jeans with long chains dangling from their pockets, hooded sweatshirts worn with big gold medallions attached to gold chains around their necks, and, of course, sneakers were key elements. The look was not just worn by hip-hop dancers; it soon spread to any young person who was a fan of hip-hop music and culture.

CHAPTER 3

Stage and Theater

Most past stars of the stage are virtually unknown today. Live theater, unlike film, is here today and gone tomorrow; however, it has still influenced our clothes. Over the past century, many new fashions have premiered in stage productions.

The prospect of the latest designer clothes on their stage idols helped pull in the audiences in the first half of the 20th century. In the latter half, since the arrival of television, musicals have hailed the latest trends from the streets and created novel looks of their own.

Left, the flamboyant Sarah Bernhardt wears one of her famous jewel-encrusted outfits from the Byzantine extravaganza *Théodora*. Right, the actress has enhanced her dramatic appearance by wearing thick eye makeup.

If people have heard of one star from the days before cinema, it is probably French actress Sarah Bernhardt, the first international superstar.

Bernhardt acted on stages from New York to Moscow. She had an exceptionally long career, debuting in Paris in the 1860s and still performing in sellout shows in the 1920s. Among her greatest roles, Marguerite in *La Dame aux Camélias* was the biggest crowd-pleaser worldwide. In this Alexandre Dumas tragedy, she plays a beautiful but gravely ill woman who finds true love before she dies. Nicknamed "the Divine Sarah," Bernhardt combined the acting gifts of an angel with a demonic capacity for outrageous behavior.

Bernhardt courted attention, and the way she dressed caused controversy on and off the stage. Defying convention, she refused to wear a corset. Newspapers of the 1880s claimed that her lavish **mantle** in *Théodora* was encrusted with so many gems that it had to be the most expensive costume ever made. In an age when the sight of a woman in trousers was truly shocking, Bernhardt played male roles and relaxed in wide-legged pants at home. She was one of the first women to openly wear makeup, and she encouraged others to do the same by advertising **rice powder**.

Sensual, mysterious, even morbid, Bernhardt notoriously slept in a coffin and kept pet snakes. By the late 19th century, the line between her private life and performances grew increasingly blurred.

Although her marvelous acting and melodramatic behavior fascinated audiences, Bernhardt's clothing was too far from the contemporary norm to inspire any major fashion trends during the 19th century. Regardless, her unique style helped prepare the way for more comfortable clothes for women in the early 1900s. Highly liberated, Bernhardt was a role model for the budding women's movement.

By the early 1900s, women's position in society was changing for the better. A wider range of socially acceptable activities was now available to women outside their homes. Women no longer needed a chaperone when they walked about on city streets. One reason for this was the growing numbers of young women employed in offices, shops, and department stores.

Almost for the first time, women could attend lectures and visit libraries or wander around parks, museums, and shops. They might dine in select restaurants alone or with friends. They were taking up energetic sports, such as cycling, tennis, and swimming. They were receiving higher education and playing a more active part in the arts, charitable work, and even politics. The calls for women's **suffrage** had never been louder, although American women had to wait until 1920 to get the vote.

SARAH BERNHARDT AND ART NOUVEAU JEWELRY

Bernhardt might not have influenced clothing design as such, but she definitely made a major contribution to fashion by popularizing Art Nouveau jewelry at the turn of the century. Art Nouveau design was mysterious and moody, full of sinuous curves and strange beauty. Bernhardt's larger-than-life personality went hand in glove with the Art Nouveau style. She looked so striking in her Art Nouveau jewels that she persuaded other women to try them, too.

Rene Lalique's twisting, curling designs were among her favorites, both on and off the stage. The greatest of all Art Nouveau goldsmiths, he crafted extraordinary jewelry incorporating unusual natural motifs, such as orchids, mistletoe, dragonflies, and bats as well as mythical creatures. Lalique used such materials as glass and horn along with valuable gold and gems to create daring effects. Some of his important pieces are more like sculptures than wearable jewelry.

Lalique abandoned goldsmithing to establish a glass company in 1909, and it is for his glass making that he is now best known.

Ethel Barrymore, another of America's foremost stage actresses, personified the "new woman." Coming to prominence on Broadway in the early 1900s, she played a series of plucky heroines, including Nora in a 1905 production of Henrik Ibsen's *A Doll's House.* In this groundbreaking drama, a woman leaves her stifling marriage to go in search of her true self. Ethel Barrymore was part of an established acting dynasty (and relatives, such as Drew Barrymore, continue to delight audiences today). Naturally graceful, Barrymore had a distinctive voice that appealed to the audiences of her day. Young women copied that voice, as well as her walk and other signature mannerisms.

As active and independent as the characters she played, Barrymore usually wore simpler clothes than many actresses of her generation, both onstage and off. She liked separates—a long skirt and a high-necked shirt with a little jacket—or a light cotton frock. Barrymore helped promote a more youthful, sportier style of dress in the early 1900s.

CHANGING THEATRICAL STYLES OF THE 1920s & 1930s

The 1920s and 1930s were the era of drawing-room comedies by such playwrights as Noel Coward, George S. Kaufman, and Moss Hart. Set in swank hotels, country houses, and stylish

About to embark on an ocean liner, Tallulah Bankhead holds a leather case for her jewelry.

38

ETHEL BARRYMORE AND FASHION DESIGNER MARIANO FORTUNY

Barrymore made another contribution to fashion. In 1922, she appeared in a lavish Broadway production of *Romeo and Juliet* that featured Mariano Fortuny's dramatic robes. It helped popularize Fortuny's designs among a wider cross section of American society.

Imported to New York from his Venice workshop, Fortuny's garments were more artworks than costumes or clothes. In the years leading up to World War I, artists and intellectuals often had one of his remarkable designs in their wardrobe to wear on casual occasions, such as entertaining close friends. Fortuny was famous for his **brocade** cloaks, simple shifts, and pleated gowns in such colors as teal blue, burnt orange, eggplant purple, and crimson. Although inspired by ancient classical robes and medieval costume, his garments had a timeless elegance that made them desirable in the fashion stores, as well as in the theater.

apartments, these plays took a witty and sophisticated look at the wealthy. Naturally, the clothes were as gorgeous as the lifestyles. They created the impression that rich women spent their entire time changing their clothes for various social engagements while making sparkling chitchat. Leading ladies, such as Gertrude Lawrence and Tallulah Bankhead, would order the latest look from leading fashion designers, such as Chanel and Jean Patou, for their roles. The accent was on fabulous evening gowns that left audiences in awe.

The latest fashions on glamorous leading ladies could pack in the audiences. Fashion designers realized that popular actresses modeling their clothes on stage was an excellent way of promoting their clothing to their target market: the theatergoing public.

In the social comedies and contemporary dramas of the 1940s, leading ladies, such as Katharine Cornell, pioneered a more tailored look. Formal eveningwear was now less likely to be seen on stage. At a time when World War II was raging in Europe and the South Pacific, buying fancy, expensive clothes to get dressed up in in the evening seemed like a frivolous thing to do, and fashions on the stage reflected this. In addition to their war work, women were also living much busier lives.

The Broadway musical *West Side Story*, a modern-day adapatation of Shakespeare's *Romeo and Juliet*, helped open the doors for fashions that came from the streets instead of the designer catwalk.

Instead, stage stars wore stylish daytime clothes, such as shirtwaist dresses, lounging robes, slacks, suits, coats, and capes. Fashion designers, such as Valentina and Hattie Carnegie, used the stage to promote comfortable shapes, both casual and glamorous, which suited American women's lifestyles. This type of tailored fashion is now known as "American sportswear."

THE EXPLOSION OF THE MUSICAL: 1940s–1960s

During the latter part of the 20th century, Broadway turned the musical into a serious art form. The story and the characters were no longer sidelined by snappy tunes and intricate footwork. The music and dance routines had to play an integral role in the plot. Performers not only had to act in between numbers, but stay in character while singing or dancing, too. The original 1943 Broadway production of *Oklahoma!* was a **watershed** and transformed the musical for good.

The costumes in *Oklahoma!* and other musicals with a frontier theme from the 1940s and 1950s, such as *Annie Get Your Gun* and *Seven Brides for Seven Brothers,* helped codify the country-and-western look. Characters' outfits included bandannas, fringed jackets, cowboy boots, cowboy hats, and skirts and shirts based on the everyday work-clothes worn by such folk in real life. People were proud of their pioneer heritage and continued to wear cowboy clothes long after the West was settled. These musicals presented a stylized, glitzy version of the Western look and helped establish what to wear to special Western events, such as rodeos and country fairs, as well as for square dancing.

By the late 1950s, young people were questioning many of their parents' beliefs and values. Teenagers started dressing in a casual style of their own. *West Side Story* picked up these street fashions and put them on the stage. The 1957 hit Broadway musical tells the story of a doomed couple torn between rival New York street gangs, a kind of updated *Romeo and Juliet.*

The girls in *West Side Story* had ponytails and dressed in full-circle skirts, narrow, fitted blouses, and shirtwaist dresses. The boys wore jeans and t-shirts or flannel shirts. The characters even talked the everyday language of the streets, dropping slang into their conversations and songs. It anticipated a more relaxed approach to language in the latter part of the 20th century.

1960s & 1970s: REFLECTIONS OF A CHANGING SOCIETY

The singer Barbra Streisand was probably the greatest star to emerge from Broadway in the second half of the 20th century. People often forget she was a stage star long before she made her first movie in 1968. That film was *Funny Girl,* and her performance was so dazzling that she won Best Actress that year at the Academy Awards. *Funny Girl* (1968) was based on the life of another stage star, vaudeville comedienne Fanny Brice. Streisand helped kick-start a fashion for **butcher's boy caps** in America in the 1960s. Later, in the 1970s, her tight corkscrew curls in *A Star Is Born* launched a fashion for crinkly perms.

Great social and political changes were underway by the late 1960s. Hippie behavior and dress implied antiestablishment values. The musical *Hair,* first performed in 1967, was a wildly successful show about this new youth culture.

For hippies, long hair was a symbol of personal freedom. Younger men grew their hair below their shoulders and wore mustaches and beards. Hippies of both sexes walked around barefoot, put on beads, and dressed in colorful clothes. They wore vivid **tie-dyed** designs, a lot of velvet, and plenty of fringes. Hippies preferred clothes from other cultures, such as Russian peasant blouses, Afghan coats, Gypsy flounced skirts, Mexican **ponchos**, Indian tunics, and Arabian **caftans**. *Hair* displayed hippie clothes in all their groovy glory. The musical played a large role in establishing a look that dominated youth fashions for the first half of the 1970s.

Another Broadway debut, *Cabaret* (1966), was overshadowed by the incredibly powerful movie of the same name. The 1972 film version, which won eight Oscars at the Academy Award ceremonies, featured Liza Minnelli's performance of a lifetime and Bob Fosse's sizzling dance routines. Set in a sleazy nightclub, the

DANSKIN AND CAPEZIO

Danskin is the name of an American range of leotards and tights first created in the 1950s. Triumph Hosiery Mills, the makers, specialized in theatrical stockings and commercial **hosiery**. Their innovative products, which appealed initially to performers, gradually crept into mainstream fashion. Crucially, Danskin theatrical tights rarely sagged at the knees or ankles. Danskin was one of the first dance ranges with colored leotards. Up until the 1950s, leotards had been almost uniformly black. Danskin introduced "Ballet Pink" and "Theatrical Pink," which are now classic shades for theatrical fashions. Danskin also introduced seamless hoisery in the 1960s and leotards with snap-crotches in the 1970s.

During the disco explosion, Danskin's up-to-date attitude helped take its styles out of the rehearsal studio and onto the dance floor. Women started wearing leotards with jeans or a matching wraparound skirt to dance clubs. This look soon spread to the streets. Danskin even produced one-piece swimsuits inspired by its bodysuits and leotards.

Capezio, another American producer of theatrical fashions, also experienced an upsurge in popularity during the disco era. Founded in the 1880s, the company originally specialized in ballet slippers and other theatrical footwear. Thanks to some input from fashion designer Clare McCardell in 1944, Capezio branched out into ballet slipper-style pumps for outdoor wear. These flat pumps, as well as button-strap, low-heeled shoes based on tap shoes, were highly fashionable in the late 1970s.

musical explores the decadence of late 1920s Berlin and Hitler's rise to power. Although Minnelli's sharp, geometric hairstyle in the film had its imitators, it was her halter-neck top that sparked off the biggest trend during the 1970s.

The original 1972 Broadway production of *Grease* was bringing in huge audiences long before Hollywood put Danny and Sandy, the central characters, on screen. The musical takes place in a 1950s high school. It is a simple "rebel boy meets good girl" story presented with lively tunes. The show delights in nostalgia for the era of **greasers** and **bobby-soxers**. Boys were dressed in white t-shirts, rolled-up jeans, and leather jackets, and used grease for slicked-back hair and a curly forelock, while girls dressed in circle skirts, twin sets, and cropped slacks and wore white bobby socks with their shoes. *Grease* tapped into a growing interest in 1950s culture and fashion, which culminated in **punk** and **preppie** clothes of the late 1970s and early 1980s.

The most successful musical of the 1970s, *A Chorus Line* had a far

A showcase for workout outfits, as well as high kicks, the Broadway musical *A Chorus Line* offered fresh ideas for exercise wear.

more inward-looking theme, in tune with the more reflective mood of the times. The entire action takes place during an audition and tells the story of the anonymous men and women who make up the supporting cast. It is all about dancing and dancers, a tribute to their lives and work.

A Chorus Line not only featured expert performances, but also the bodysuits, tights, leotards, leggings, and other clothes dancers normally work in when they are not in costume on stage. It gave women plenty of fresh ideas for what to wear when they were exercising and working out.

1980s–2000

It is hard to believe, but *Cats*—the hit 1980s musical about singing felines with quirky personalities—started a popular trend. Members of the *Cats'* cast used imaginative makeup to turn themselves into our furry friends. Suddenly, at fairgrounds and amusement parks, everyone wanted their faces painted with leopard's spots instead of clown's

This performer in *Cats* is wearing tights and leggings that were made popular by dancers in the late 1970s and early 1980s. Note the performer's makeup, creating a feline face.

smiles. At Halloween, there were more lions and tigers than monsters and ghosts knocking on doors. Cat face-painting—with whiskers—was all the rage, especially if you were under 10 years of age.

Andrew Lloyd Webber and Tim Rice, the duo that brought *Cats* to the stage, had another unlikely success with *Evita*—the rags-to-riches musical biography of Eva Perón, the glamorous wife of Argentinean dictator Juan Perón. Her magnetic personality bewitched the nation as she almost single-handedly engineered her husband's rise to power in the 1940s.

As First Lady of Argentina, Eva Perón dressed in the best Parisian **haute couture**. Immaculately groomed, she looked so regal that Argentineans treated her like a queen. Various leading ladies, including Elaine Page, Patti LuPone, and Madonna, have played Eva Perón on stage or in film.

Evita had a big impact on 1980s fashion. Designers picked up on Eva Perón's suits, with their big shoulder pads and narrow fitted waists. Women copied her trademark sleek hairstyle with a knot at the nape of the neck. *Evita*-style strapless evening gowns were seen at every dinner-dance.

Eva Perón, the real life inspiration behind the musical *Evita*, looks every inch a first lady of fashion. Pictured here with her husband, Argentine president Juan Perón.

CHAPTER 4

Circus Fun and Vaudeville

Circus and variety-show performers have not had quite the same impact on what we wear as have the more widely watched actors or dancers. Nevertheless, they have made an enormous contribution to costume design.

The word *circus* derives from a Latin term used to describe a circuit for mass entertainment. Shows at ancient Roman circuses were often spectacular and bloody, as such movies as *Ben Hur* (1959) and *Gladiator* (2000) demonstrate. However, the Romans also loved the theater, which is where some of the earliest clowns performed.

Swinging on the trapeze is dangerous. Trapeze artists, such as this girl from the Wenatchee Youth Circus (left), often use a safety wire. This jester in a colorful costume (right), with the ears of an ass on his hood, is a typical medieval entertainer.

Performers in Roman theater wore masks to indicate their characters' feelings. This is the origin of the instantly recognizable comic and tragic faces we still celebrate in circus and pantomime today.

In medieval times, entertainers traveled from town to town, playing music, singing, dancing, acting, tumbling, juggling, and performing tricks. They dressed in the colorful clothes we now associate with the circus. The luckiest had positions in kings' palaces and the homes of nobility. Jesters, or fools, are the best-known of these entertainers. They were as flexible as they were funny, combining acrobatics with humor. Jesters wore hoods and pointed shoes decorated with tinkling bells. They dressed in striped coats and brightly colored hose. The jester's costume was a major influence on the appearance of today's clowns. On the way, clowns' costumes have gradually evolved through a whole series of memorable characters. One of these is Pickelherring, a popular character in 17th- and 18th-century German comic theater. Pickelherring and his pals dressed in oversized shoes, floppy hats, baggy vests, and big ruffled collars.

The modern clown's white makeup comes from 18th-century French comic theater. The first celebrated "white-faced" clown was an early 19th-century English entertainer named Joseph Grimaldi. He looked and behaved just like a modern clown. Even today, clowns are still called "Joey" as a tribute to this great clown. Another famous 19th-century clown, Dan Rice, was the model for one of America's great patriotic images. Rice's clown had a blue coat, red and white trousers, a top hat, and a little goatee beard. "Yankee Dan" became "Uncle Sam."

THE MODERN CIRCUS

The modern circus as we recognize it today got its start in the late 1760s, thanks to an English riding instructor. Philip Astley began performing tricks upon horseback outside his London school to attract students. He quickly realized he had stumbled on a hit. Astley began charging admission and recruited clowns, jugglers, and tightrope walkers to entertain the crowds in

COMMEDIA DEL'ARTE

Commedia del'arte is an Italian form of comedy popular throughout Europe in the 17th and 18th centuries. The format is based on a set of characters who always dress and behave the same way and in which all the characters, apart from a pair of lovers, wear masks.

The acrobatic clown, Harlequin, is probably the best-known *commedia del'arte character*. He dresses in a colorful diamond-patched suit and a black mask, while his girlfriend, Columbine, wears a similar patchwork dress. Harlequin always carries a baton to hit characters that annoy him—the origin of the term *slapstick*, which has come to mean physical-action comedy.

Another well-known *commedia del'arte* character is sad, lovesick Pierrot. He dresses in a loose white suit with a ruffled collar and skullcap. Pierrot originally wore a white mask, but this was later changed to white makeup.

From the turn of the 20th century to the 1930s, dressing up as Harlequin and Pierrot was popular with musicians and men going to costume balls. The two characters also inspired advertising posters and ceramic figurines.

between riding tricks. The show became so popular that Astley built an arena with a circular grandstand so that audiences could get a better view. However, this type of entertainment was not called a circus until the 1780s, when Charles Hughes opened a rival arena, which he called "The Royal Circus," after the ancient Roman model to give his shows cultural flavor.

In the early 19th century, many big cities had permanent circus arenas, while a downscaled version of the circus traveled to small country towns. The "big top" tent was invented in the 1820s, but circuses did not grow to today's extravagant proportions until the mid-19th century, when the new railroads could transport them easily from place to place. Once they arrived at their destination, performers held a parade to let people know the circus had come to town.

Throughout the 19th century, riding was the main circus attraction. Today's master of ceremonies at the circus—the ringmaster—once controlled the horses so the riders could concentrate on their tricks. This is why ringmasters still dress in old-fashioned riding clothes. Their traditional outfit consists of tan **breeches**, black riding boots, a red tailcoat, a black top hat, and a white **cravat**, shirt, and vest.

On November 12, 1859, a daring new act debuted at the Cirque Napoléon in Paris. High above the audience, a performer leapt from one swinging bar to another, and the flying trapeze was born. Ironically, this famous routine's inventor, Jules Léotard, is better remembered today thanks to his bodysuit costume. The original leotard was made of wool and modestly

In a circus-themed production of the opera *The Bartered Bride,* this singer's costume immediately establishes that he is the ringmaster.

extended halfway down the thigh. It quickly caught on and became the standard working costume for circus performers, as well as for dancers.

Today, many circus costumes follow these time-honored models, except that modern costumes are perhaps brighter and flashier than older ones. Current performers wear the shiniest satins, electric colors, and sequins. Modern circus costumes are also more comfortable to perform in, because they are made from the latest technologically advanced materials, such as stretchy Lycra and spandex, instead of the wool and silk used in the past.

Nonetheless, each country with a circus tradition has given rise to its own individually designed costumes and identifiable acts. For example, the Russian circus is legendary for its flexible acrobats and matchless clowns. Russians are justifiably proud of their circus performers and regard them as highly skilled, creative artists on a par with ballet dancers and opera stars. Russian circus performers frequently wear costumes inspired by national folk dress. Male performers wear wide pantaloon trousers tucked into boots, collarless shirts, and round fur hats; the women wear red boots, short peasant skirts, and kerchiefs on their heads.

The Chinese circus developed separately from the Western circus. Many traditional routines are over 2,000 years old. The Chinese circus is admired for its acrobats—tumbling, jumping through hoops, and balancing on long bamboo poles—and jugglers spinning plates on long sticks. A recent favorite is the bicycling act, in which improbable numbers of people all ride on the same bicycle at the same time.

Chinese circus performers generally dress in colorful costumes based on traditional Chinese dress. Tops have flared sleeves and fasten with frog closers made from loops of braid. Pants are cropped just above the ankle, and many performers wear flat-soled, button-up Chinese slippers.

The Chinese circus' most unusual act, the lion dance, has unique costumes that set it apart. The lion dance requires great coordination and acrobatic skill

These Chinese acrobats from Shanghai prefer dazzling leotards in turquoise and white to traditional costumes. The troop has just won an award for their sensational tumbling at the Monte Carlo International Circus Festival.

on the part of the performers inside the lion's costume. This dance has ancient Buddhist roots. In China, the lion is a good-luck symbol that protects against evil. There are two kinds of lion costume in the Chinese circus. Northern Chinese lions have large golden heads with big eyes and bodies with long fur, while southern Chinese lions are more comical, with splashes of bright color on their bodies.

The award-winning Canadian troupe Cirque du Soleil brings a contemporary twist to the circus scene. Founded in Quebec in 1984, Cirque du Soleil grew out of a company of street performers, and since then, they have entertained millions worldwide. There are no animals in Cirque du Soleil productions. Their themed shows combine traditional circus acrobatics, street performance, magical lighting effects, and rock music. Their sets are spectacular and their costumes wild. Cirque du Soleil performers often wear all-in-one bodysuits that cover them from head to toe.

VARIETY SHOWS

The circus and variety shows had a lot more in common than clowns and juggling. Both brought mass entertainment to people from all walks of life and used a well-tested formula that featured a sequence of unconnected acts, each created and presented by performers specializing in their own function. Both helped bring such terms as *billboard*, *top of the bill*, and *top billing* into common use.

Variety shows featured a little bit of everything, from music and dancing to comedy and specialty acts, such as celebrity speakers or ice skating. Called "vaudeville" in America and "music hall" in Britain, it was the most popular form of entertainment between 1870 and 1930. In the days before movies and radio became commonplace, most small towns in America had their own theater with a variety show.

Comedy acts were a big feature of variety shows. In fact, many of today's stock characters and standard comic routines were first introduced in variety shows. There is the tramp, personified by Charlie Chaplin with his little mustache, bowler hat, and cane; or the drunk, personified by W. C. Fields with his checkered trousers and bulbous nose. There are double acts in which comedians play off each other, such as Laurel and Hardy or Abbott and Costello. There is also the ventriloquist, who can speak without moving his lips so that it looks like his wooden sidekick is saying outrageous things.

Variety was also responsible for establishing many of our entertainment idioms and costume clichés. Barbershop quartets—four men singing old-fashioned songs in harmony—normally dress in striped jackets, white flannel slacks, and straw hats. Magicians wear top hats, tailcoats, and capes with red linings. Conjurers dress in turbans and brightly colored robes. The strongman bares one shoulder in his leopard-skin costume and carries a huge barbell.

Musical revue is an offshoot of variety shows. The idea originally came from Paris' Folies-Bergère, which featured comedy acts, song-and-dance numbers, and sketches, as well as chorus lines. What made musical revue different from ordinary variety was an overall theme or a rudimentary story line. There was a single cast, and each routine was specifically created to form part of a particular show. Musical revues were legendary for their lavish sets and glamorous costumes.

However, when it came to extravagant musical revues, nobody could top Florenz Ziegfeld. The Ziegfeld Follies, his no-expense-spared production, ran annually in New York from 1907 to 1932. Ziegfeld only worked with the best. He employed comedians, such as Fanny Brice and W. C. Fields, and featured dancers, such as Gilda Gray, whose life was captured in the film *Gilda* (1946), starring Rita Hayworth. Famous composers, such as Irving Berlin and Jerome Kern, wrote Ziegfeld's music.

Ziegfeld girls wore the most fantastic finery—in fact, it was widely believed at the time that some of the girls held their place more on their looks than their talent. So important were the costumes in musical revue—and one

Film star Charlie Chaplin got his start in British variety theater. His interpretation of a "little tramp" is one of the most instantly recognizable and beloved of all 20th-century comic characters.

PANTOMIME

Pantomime is traditional English family entertainment at Christmas. Featuring extravagant sets and spectacular costumes, today's noisy pantomimes evolved from 17th- and 18th-century mimed slapstick comedy. Humorous plots are loosely based on classic fairy tales, such as Cinderella. Many of the jokes have double meanings that are sometimes risqué. Audience participation is a must. They cheer the "goodies" and jeer at the "baddies," using a repertoire of traditional phrases, such as "He's behind you!" to warn the unsuspecting hero.

In pantomime, the hero is called a principal boy—but, confusingly, is played by a girl. She wears shorts, bright-colored tights, and thigh-length, high-heeled boots. In standard pantomime plot, the principal boy rescues a beautiful heroine from a "baddie" and marries her. The principal boy is supported by an outrageous character called a dame, who is always a man obviously dressed up to look like woman in gaudy clothes. Widow Twankey, Aladdin's mother, is the most famous of all the pantomime dames.

of the main reasons why audiences came to see the shows—that their job was to look fabulous in the show's costumes, more like today's catwalk models.

Among the many costume designers who worked for Ziegfeld, Erté is probably the best remembered today. Popular in the 1920s and 1930s, he was one of the most renowned **Art Deco** designers. His luxurious style, inspired by Oriental and African designs, was expressed using geometric and stylized shapes. Erté created the most fantastical outfits for the Zeigfeld Follies. Garlands of pearls, bold jewelry, and extravagant plumed headdresses were hallmarks of his style. Erté also worked as a fashion illustrator, and fashion magazines, such as *Vogue* and *Harper's Bazaar,* published his colored drawings.

CHORUS LINES

The idea of a chorus line first came from the can-can dancers who entertained at Parisian music halls, such as the Moulin Rouge, in the 19th century. Lines of girls in frilly petticoats, all high-kicking together, were familiar worldwide by the early 1900s. Also around the same time, the Englishman John Tiller began featuring lines of girls dancing and marching together in his own amateur shows. It was such a success that he started training and providing "Tiller Girls" for revues and variety shows internationally. Now know as precision dancing, many of Tiller's arrangements are still in use today.

Other dance troupes soon adopted the Tiller Girls' uniform style. America's best-known chorus line, the Rockettes, started dancing at Radio City Music Hall in New York in 1932. Many of the famous routines have never been altered, and the Rockettes are still kicking together today.

Chorus-line costumes have changed very little since those early days. Chorus dancers continue to dress identically in shiny bodysuits with plenty of sparkles and feathers. Towering headdresses and low-heeled satin shoes with straps are other features of the chorus-line look.

GLOSSARY

Art Deco a stark, classical style expressed using geometric and stylized shapes

Art Nouveau literally means "new art" in French; characterized by sinuous lines, tendril motifs, and moody and mysterious figures

Bias cutting garments made of fabrics cut across the woven grain, so they are both comfortable and clingy at the same time; bias-cut gowns were very popular in the 1930s

Bobby-soxers American teenage girls who wore white ankle socks with their shoes in 1950s; other bobby-soxer fashions include circle skirts, loafers, twin sets, and ponytails

Breeches short pants covering the hips and thighs and fitting snugly at the lower edges at or just below the knee

Brocade a fabric characterized by raised designs

Brogues flat-heeled, lace-up shoes usually decorated with thick stitching and tiny circular perforations originally worn by men.

Butcher's-boy cap a cap with a large brim based on a 19th-century deliveryman's cap

Caftan a usually cotton or silk ankle-length garment with long sleeves

Chaps pant coverings worn by cowboys for protection against dust and thorny branches; usually made of leather, suede, or fur

Cravat a necktie

Crinoline a cage of wire hoops worn under long skirts, like a petticoat, to give them extraordinary girth

Diamanté a faceted glass or plastic stone that resembles a diamond

Epaulets shoulder straps or ornaments on military coats or jackets; also used to decorate civilian coats and jackets

Greasers teenaged punks in the 1950s who wore black leather jackets, t-shirts, rolled-up jeans, and hair slicked back with grease

Harem pants wide-legged pants that are tight at the ankle; inspired by garments worn by women in the Orient

Haute couture the houses or designers that create exclusive and often trend-setting fashions; also the fashions created there

Hedonist a person who believes that pleasure or happiness is the sole or chief good in life

Hobble skirt a long skirt that is narrow

below the knee, forcing the wearer to take tiny steps

Hosiery collectively, stockings, pantyhose, tights, and socks

Jersey a close-fitting, usually circular-knitted, garment especially for the upper body

Lamé fabric woven with flat metallic threads

Lampshade dress a dress with a tunic overtop that has been stiffened at the base in a circular shape so it resembles a lampshade

Mantle a full, hooded cloak, often embroidered and trimmed with tassels

Motif theme

Pirouette a full turn on the toe or ball of one foot in ballet

Poncho a woolen square with an opening in the center so it can be pulled over the head and worn like a cape, originally from Mexico

Preppie American collegiate outfits of the 1950s inspired this popular 1980s trend; preppies dressed in fashion classics, such as blazers, Shetland sweaters, penny loafers, plaid skirts, and button-down shirts

Punk an anti-establishment street style from the late 1970s, which included black leather jackets, spiked hair, ripped jeans and t-shirts, and safety pin decoration. Later in the 1980s some punk ideas found their way into mainstream fashions

Rice powder a facial powder used to make complexions paler

Shift a usually loose-fitting or semifitted dress

Snood a lacy hair accessory popular in the late 1930s and 1940s used to hold hair in a large bun at the nape of the neck

Spur a pointed device secured to a rider's heel and used to urge on the horse

Suffrage the right of voting

Tie-dye decorative patterns on fabric created by tying up sections so they remain untouched by the dying process

Tulle a crisp, see-through fabric used mainly for decorating dresses, skirts, and hats

Tutu a short, projecting skirt worn by a ballerina

Twin set a matching set of pullover sweater and cardigan

Watershed a crucial dividing point, line, or factor

TIMELINE

1900–1910 First regular radio broadcasts; first commercial gramophone records released on shellac discs; start of the commercial motion-picture industry, mainly in France and the United States.

1914 Outbreak of World War I in Europe.

1917 U.S. enters World War I.

1918 WWI armistice.

1920 Women win the vote; Marconi sets up first public radio station.

1923 The Charleston dance craze.

1927 Al Jolson stars in *The Jazz Singer*, the first widely distributed "talkie" (movie with sychronized dialogue on the soundtrack).

1929 Wall Street Crash, followed by the Great Depression.

1931 First regular television broadcasts.

1932 Adrian's designs for Joan Crawford in *Letty Lynton* are widely copied.

1935 First live-action color film *La Cucharacha* (U.S.) released.

1938 Vivien Leigh cast as Scarlett O'Hara in *Gone with the Wind,* one of the most popular movies of all time.

1939–1945 World War II.

1941 U.S. enters World War II.

1946 Jukebox boom in U.S. and U.K.

1947 Paris fashion designer Christian Dior introduces "New Look."

1955 James Dean stars in *Rebel Without a Cause.*

1957 *West Side Story*, by Leonard Bernstein, opens on Broadway.

1960 John F. Kennedy elected president.

1967 *Bonnie and Clyde* is released, and *Hair* debuts on Broadway.

1969 Woodstock becomes a major music festival, with 400,000 attending; Neil Armstrong first man on the moon.

1972 Film version of musical *Cabaret* sweeps Academy Awards.

1975 *A Chorus Line* debuts on Broadway.

1977 Ralph Lauren creates the casual, layered chic look for Diane Keaton in *Annie Hall.*

1978 *Dallas* debuts on TV.

1979 Sony, in Japan, launches the Walkman.

1982 Rap music takes off in U.S. and U.K.

1985 Live Aid concert, with worldwide TV audience of 1.5 billion, raises $52 million for Ethiopian famine victims.

2002 Halle Berry is first black woman to win Best Actress Academy Award for *Monster's Ball.*

FURTHER INFORMATION

BOOKS

Driver, Ian. *A Century of Dance.* London: Hamlyn, 2000.

Ewing, Elizabeth. *History of 20th Century Fashion (revised edition).* New York: Quite Specific Media Group Ltd., 2002.

Proddow, Penny, Debra Healy and Marion Fasel. *Hollywood Jewels.* New York: Harry N. Abrams, 1992.

Tapert, Annette. *The Power of Glamour.* London: Aurum Press, 1999.

ONLINE SOURCES

Artslynx International Dance Resources
www.artslynx.org/dance/index.htm
Excellent links to ballet and dance resources available online.

Clown Ministry
www.clown-ministry.com/index.html
Dedicated to the history and performance of clowning, this Web site provides in-depth information about different types of clowns,

their genealogy, makup, costumes, and even the clown "pecking order."

Cyber Encyclopedia of Musical Theater, TV, and Film
www.musicals101.com/variety101.html
Essays on American variety, minstrel shows, British music hall, vaudeville, and burlesque, plus chronologies and a useful guide to related links and bibliography.

ABOUT THE AUTHOR

Alycen Mitchell holds an MA in 19th-century art and design from the University of London. She writes and lectures on the decorative arts, specializing in jewelry and fashion. As an author, she has contributed to

many publications, from *The Financial Post* and *Management Consultancy* to *Antique Dealer, Collectors Guide,* and the art and antiques Web site www.icollector.com.

INDEX

References in italics refer to illustrations

accessories
    bags 19, 24, *38*
    gloves 18, 24, 28
    leg warmers 30, 46
    scarves 19, 21
Art Nouveau 24, 37
Astaire, Fred 28–9

Baker, Josephine 27–8
Barrymore, Ethel 38, 39
beards 42, 50
beatniks *16,* 17, 19
Bernhardt, Sarah *34, 36,* 37
Bow, Clara *9,* 12
Broadway 14, 38

Castle, Irene 26–7, 29
Chaplin, Charlie 55, *56*
cinema
    Academy Awards 21
    silent movies 9–12
    Westerns *10,* 11
circuses *48,* 49, 50–5
clowns 49, 50, 51, 53
colors 26, 32, 39, 42, 43,
    50, 53, 57
costumes *see also* menswear;
    underwear; womenswear
    ballet *22,* 25, 26, *31*
    chorus girls 58, *59*
    circuses 52–5
    clowns 50, 51
    cowboys *10,* 11, 41
    disco 32, 43
    ethnic 42, 53
    eveningwear 12–14, *16,*
    24, 28–9, 32, 39, 40, 47
    flappers 27
    Hispanic 29, 33
    jazz dancing 27–8
    modern dancing *23,*
    24–5, 29, 30
    musical revues 56–7
    rehearsal wear 30, 43,
    44–5, 46
    street dancing 32–3
    vamps 10–11

dancing
    ballet *22,* 25, 26, 30, *31*
    ballroom 24, 26–7, 28–9
    can-can *58–9*
    Charleston 27
    chorus lines 58, *59*
    disco 30, 32
    Hispanic 29, 33
    jazz 27–8, 30
    lion 53–4
    modern 23–5, 29, 30
    street 32–3
designers 26, 27, 32, 37
    cinema costumes 14, 18,
    21
    stage costumes 39, 57
dresses *see also* womenswear
    ballet *22, 23,* 31
    crinolines 15
    evening 12–14, *16,* 24,
    28–9, 39, 40, 47
    lampshade 26, 27
    shifts 12, 39
    shirtwaists 41
Duncan, Isadora 23–6, 29

Eastern influence 25, 26

fabrics
    bias-cut *8,* 13–14
    gold lamé 17, 26
    manmade fibers 53
    satin 26, 32, 53
    silk 26, 32, 53
    velvet 26, 42
footwear
    ballet shoes 19, 25, 31, 43
    boots 52, 53, 57
    shoes *13,* 17, 30, 43, 45,
    50, 53
    sneakers 33

Gish, Lillian 9–10
Grant, Cary 12

hairstyles 24, 30, 41, 42, 43,
    45, 47
    bobs *9,* 12, 27, 28
    cinema *9, 10,* 12, 17–18,
    19
    Harlow, Jean 13–14
headgear

berets 20
caps 27, 42
hats 18, 21, 30, 50, 52,
    53, 55
headdresses 14, 25, 27, 58
hoods *49,* 50
top hats *28,* 52, 55
turbans 11, 17, 26, 55
Hepburn, Audrey 19
Hepburn, Katharine *13,*
    14–15

jeans 11, 17, 30, 32, 33, 43,
    45
jesters *49,* 50
jewelry 17, 19, 24, 26, 27–8,
    33, 37, 57

Kelly, Grace 18–19

makeup *8, 9,* 11, 12, 32, *35,*
    36, 46–7
    clowns 50, 51
masks 50, 51
menswear *see also* costumes
    coats 15, 50
    jackets 14, 17, 55
    leather jackets 11, 45
    shirts 11, 12, 32, 53
    t-shirts 17, 33, 45
    tailcoats 26, 28, 52, 55
    trousers 30, 32, 55
    tuxedos 12
    zoot suits 30
Miranda, Carmen 17
movies *see* cinema
music
    country and western *10,*
    11, 27–8
    jazz 27–8
    music hall 55–6
    musical revue 56–7
    musicals 11, 35, *40,* 41–7

pantomimes 57
Paris 24, 25–6, 28, 47
Perón, Eva 47
Pickford, Mary 9–10

Rogers, Ginger 28–9
Rogers, Roy *10,* 11

shoulder pads 14, 47

skirts 17, 19, 25, 38, 53
    see also womenswear
    circle 41, 45
    hobble 26, 27
    tutu 22, 25, 31
    wraparound 32, 43
sportswear 33, 41
street fashions *40,* 41–2
Streisand, Barbra 42
swimwear 43

teenagers 41
trapeze artists *48,* 52

underwear *see also*
    womenswear
    corsets 21, 24, 36
    tights 43, *46,* 57

variety shows 55–6

women's liberation 36–8
womenswear *see also*
    accessories; costumes;
    dresses; skirts; underwear
    blouses 41
    cloaks 36, 39, 41
    coats 19, 26, 41
    harem pants 26
    kimonos 26
    leotards 32, 43, 52–3
    shirts 19, 38
    suits 38, 41, 47
    trousers *13,* 14–15, 19,
    21, 36, 41
    twin sets 19, 45
World War I 25, 27
World War II 40

Ziegfeld, Florenz 56–7